The Rites of Passage for Males Manual

Just About Everything a Young Man Needs to Know about Life and Manhood

D. Harold Greene

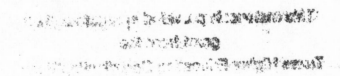

Hamilton Books

A member of
THE ROWMAN & LITTLEFIELD PUBLISHING GROUP
Lanham • Boulder • New York • Toronto • Plymouth, UK

Copyright © 2008 by
Hamilton Books
4501 Forbes Boulevard
Suite 200
Lanham, Maryland 20706
Hamilton Books Acquisitions Department (301) 459-3366

Estover Road
Plymouth PL6 7PY
United Kingdom

Library of Congress Control Number: 2007942772
ISBN-13: 978-0-7618-3942-2 (paperback : alk. paper)
ISBN-10: 0-7618-3942-9 (paperback : alk. paper)

Contents

Foreword

To my son,

This manual is for you because I know that you need answers to help you to learn how to take care of yourself and how to survive in this tough world. You are not by yourself as this is a problem that many young men, such as yourself, will face as they mature and become adults.

This book will help you to understand manhood based on the life experiences of other men who have been through what you are going through now. From their life experiences, you will get answers to what you need to know about life and what it takes to be a man.

You learned the hard way that the world will react in a negative way to your negative actions. You must decide now to take a positive and responsible approach to your manhood.

As you move through your teen years, you have questioned everything that you have learned from me. This is necessary to help you to formulate your own options for your adult life. In time, everything that you have learned from other men will come together to mold you into a focused, dedicated and responsible man.

As you approach manhood, remember that the keys to overcoming the challenges and struggles of life are listening and learning. If you can master these skills, then there will be nothing in life that you cannot accomplish.

With love, I dedicate this book, *The Rites of Passage for Males Manual*, to you.

Rites of Passage History

IT BEGAN IN AFRICA

In Africa, as a young man approaches the age of maturity—thirteen or fourteen—he is expected to prepare to enter into manhood which includes such responsibilities as hunting, taking part in male activities in the village, gathering firewood, helping to build and repair village huts and guarding the village. At this age of maturity, he immediately becomes a warrior to fight in the tribal wars along with the other men.

At the age of maturity, he is required to move from his father's and mother's home, and he is required to build a home for himself. On completion of his home, he would be prepared to choose a wife and to start a family.

The Rite of Passage was a three-day ritual to honor and to welcome young men of the village to the world of manhood, with all the rights and privileges that come with being a man.

WHAT WE ARE EXPECTED TO DO AS MEN

Among those rights and privileges are respect and honor from everyone in the village. To maintain these rights and privileges, entrance into manhood also requires discipline and responsibility.

WHAT THE WORLD THINKS OF US

Discipline requires a forthright effort to learn and to educate oneself to be a better man. Responsibility requires that a man obey all the rules and laws of the village. He must also respect his elders, especially his father and mother.

It is unfortunate that in today's society, urban males are not as highly regarded as the young warriors in Africa. As young men approach the age of maturity in this country, they project an image of being just the opposite of what is required of a young African warrior. This image is destructive.

Chapter One

Basic Life Skills

TAKING CARE OF OURSELVES

Life is real! Even when we are asleep, life goes on. It never stops. Every day we must get up and show up for life. Some days are harder than others. Some days are more fun than others. But we, as men, must show up. We will not always be successful when we show up, but one thing is for sure, if we don't get up and show up, there will be no success for us.

There will be no win. Even if we won today, yesterday or two days ago, we still have to show up the rest of the week, because today's score will not win tomorrow's ballgame.

You will not win every time you get up, but you'll never win if you don't get up and play the game of life. What you did yesterday won't make you a winner today. Yesterdays win helps to build your confidence and improve

1

your skills, but you have to take that confidence and those improved skills to the court every day in order to enjoy a successful life.

Showing up is only half the battle of being a man. The never-ending journey through life requires that you, as a man, learn to take care of yourself. This journey is yours and you are the one who has to get up every day, show up and get on with your life despite any obstacles that might get into your way.

In most instances, if there is a problem, you are often responsible for that problem, but even if you are not, you must be responsible for solving it. You can't run and you can't hide, as a problem seldom goes away. You must take care of it, and you must take care of yourself.

Quite often, you will take some wrong turns. You will become confused about what is right. You will think that the number of women you have, your wealth, and how manly you are or look, measures your worth as a man. You will find that your popularity with women, having lots of money and being successful in sports or your career are not the true marks of manhood.

You should define manhood as "the ability to overcome obstacles in the path that leads to success in life." Continuing to step up to the plate despite all obstacles is the manly trait. Sticking in there. Taking responsibility for what you say or do is key. Never giving up, because if you do, you lose.

What is right is right, what is wrong is wrong. You must determine what is right for you and what is wrong for you. Make that decision and move forward in this game of life. Remember, life is a game. There are winners and there are losers. You must determine which you would prefer to be.

Surviving day-to-day is a challenge. There will be many things that will get you upset and worried. Don't depend on others to do what you have to do for yourself. Take charge of your life. Be a man.

SELF-DEFEATING BEHAVIOR

Nothing drives men crazy—or makes us hate ourselves more—than to realize that we have been keeping ourselves from gaining the love, success and happiness we want in our lives. That is what self-defeating behavior does. It works against our own best interests and it defies your deepest desires. It creates more problems than it can solve. That is why, when you catch yourself doing something wrong, you may want to scream, "I can't believe I did that!" and "I should know better! I'm my own worst enemy!"

How many times have you said those words to yourself? Also, how many times have you identified exactly how you are defeating yourself, and then vow to never do it again?

The first thing that you need to know is that you are not alone. Most people have been in your shoes and gone through a period in their life where they have felt foolish because of self-defeating behavior. Remember, some people even figure out how to change but then they don't follow through.

WHY WE DEFEAT OURSELVES

Self-defeating behavior occurs when we fail to learn the lessons that life teaches us. It represents impulse over awareness, immediate gratification over lasting satisfaction and relief over resolution. Think about this. Have you ever done something on impulse without considering the consequences of your actions? That is usually self-defeating behavior. You do things out of control that will affect your life in both a positive or, in most instances, in a negative way.

Self-defeating behavior usually begins as an attempt to make yourselves feel better. It is a coping mechanism. When faced with a crisis, a threat or a potentially upsetting situation, you try to protect yourself. You look for something that will reduce tension or keep you from getting hurt. This action makes sense to you, and it may offer some short-term relief, but self-defeating behavior often come back to haunt us.

Although you feel stupid, foolish, and weak when you do these crazy things, the fact is you were simply responding to a threatening or confusing situation without first considering the alternatives to such self-defeating acts and behavior.

You have to develop a coping mechanism; recognize the root causes of your self-defeating actions and behavior. For instance, if you were abused during your youth and teen years, you may experience anger and strike out at the world in the face of an adverse or difficult situation. If you were neglected during your youth and teen years, you may tend to feel defeated and withdraw from situations that challenge you.

Surviving day-to-day is a definite challenge. The most important thing you can do to overcome self-defeating behavior is to obtain love, encouragement, and effective guidance from your support group—family, positive friends, teachers or mentors. That will help you develop healthy coping mechanisms with adverse or difficult situations that confront you.

You need to learn to be resilient, confident and resourceful in the midst of threatening or confusing situations. There will be many things that will get you upset and worried. Don't depend on others to do what you have to do for yourself.

HOW TO DEFEAT SELF-DEFEATING BEHAVIOR

Self-defeating behaviors are usually bad reactions. We normally act without regard for long-term consequences and without considering reasonable alternatives. Here are some basic steps to help you to choose the best course of action when facing daily challenges, instead of acting on impulse:

Step 1: Stop and notice what you feel about your problem or situation and where you feel it.

Step 2: Ask yourself, "Why do I feel tense? What do I feel angry about? What am I afraid of?"

Step 3: Do these feelings make you want to take action? What actions are you about to take?

Step 4: Ask yourself what the short-term and long-term consequences will be if I take this action?

Step 5: Ask yourself, "If this action is self-defeating, what alternatives do I have to this action?"

Step 6: Ask yourself, "Can I discuss this problem or situation with someone whom I am comfortable in sharing my problem or situation with, and whom can help to resolve the situation I am in?"

GET SOME HELP

Since self-defeating behavior may be due to your childhood experience of being alone and helpless, it is easier to overcome in adulthood if you get support from others.

You need a support person or group to talk to and give you advice and counsel. You also need someone to provide moral support and to hold you accountable for the decisions that you make. Most important, you need to know that you are not alone. This will strengthen you confidence and determination.

SURVIVING SETBACKS

Surviving day-to-day is sometimes a real challenge. There will be many set-backs in your daily life journey. Self-defeating behavior usually repeats itself. Despite your best efforts to change your behavior, the same or similar situations or problems may pop up again and you might do the same self-defeating action as you did before.

If you have a setback, don't beat-up on yourself because you made the same mistake; convert your self-disappointment into self-determination. Review what you did this time and make a determined decision that if this situation happens again, decide what you can do that is not self-defeating the next time. Develop a plan of action for a similar problem or situation, and carry it out the next time.

COMMITTING TO CHANGE

It is not easy to admit that you have been keeping yourself from gaining the love, success and happiness you want in your lives. Blaming your problems on other people, or on circumstances beyond your control, doesn't make any-thing better in your life. You alone have the power to change your life and the situations that you put yourself in.

Taking responsibility for your own actions is crucial if you are going to beat the self-destructive habits of self-defeating behavior. Yes, self-destruct! That is what self-defeating behavior does. It works against your best interests and it will make you fail in everything that you try to do. It just creates more problems for you. You can stop self-defeating behavior. Do it NOW!

GETTING INVOLVED WITH THE WRONG PEOPLE

Finding the right people to be with is a challenging. It may be the most diffi-cult task that you will encounter in your life. It is like trying to find a ripe ap-ple without first taking a bite. Unlike rotten apples, rotten people often bite us first.

So how do you avoid the pitfalls of choosing friends, business associates, mentors, girl friends, mates or even family member who are the right peo-ple to be with? First, learn to identify the wrong people. There are several examples.

The Taker

Takers impress you with power, charisma (beauty) and/or strength. If you feel powerless, you may want to be around them because it makes you feel powerful or strong. Don't be fooled by their hype. They get their power and strength by sucking it out of others. They are takers. They know how to make you feel loved or special. It feels good at first because they haven't started to hurt you yet. They will before long.

The Needy

You are drawn to these people because they need you—money, sex or love, etc.. You want to be with them and treat them the way you want to be treated. It makes you feel important. They seem unthreatening and incapable of hurting you, but they are also incapable of giving much to you.

You think that you can change these people into the type of person that you want, but in most instances, they simply drain you. If this happens, you may feel used, and used up, and you could become cold, aloof and maybe even abuse them.

With either type, your best intentions may defeat you in the end. To avoid this outcome, you need to identify the individual's core personality. This helps you to understand how to deal with him or her without being hurt. Those people to be wary of have either a core-of-hate personality or a core-of-hurt personality.

CORE OF HATE PERSONALITY

These people are at war with the world and everything in it. They often seem to be very nice and charming people at first, but watch out, because they are really competitive (I've got to have the best), adversarial (Don't tell me what to do!), and usually belligerent (You are no good, you don't have anything to offer me!). Perhaps you have met this type of person. They can turn every disagreement into a confrontation and quickly try to gain the upper hand. When you are with them, you will end up feeling wrong or inferior.

People with the core-of-hate personality can't stand to lose. It is as if they were so badly hurt or abused as a child that they may have vowed to always have their way when they became adults. You don't need this kind of relationship from a friend, lover or associate. You can become so afraid of getting hurt that you may sacrifice your own needs and goals to keep them satisfied.

If you tell a person with the core-of-hate personality your goals and aspirations, you may have to fight a battle of wills as he or she tries to deflate your enthusiasm and to sabotage you efforts. These people are often self-centered, perhaps even scornful. They can destroy your dreams and ambitions (if you let them) with negative words and actions.

How to Deal with a Core-of-Hate Personality

- If you can't avoid them, accept that you can't change them.
- Don't become too intimate or trusting.
- Don't compete with them. You can't win with people who won't lose. Even if you gain a victory, they won't let you enjoy it.
- Don't be intimidated or get deterred from your goals or dreams.
- Don't argue or debate with them; just think of a fair and reasonable course of action, and follow it.

CORE-OF-HURT PERSONALITY

These people are more frustrating than hurtful. Being with them is very shaky. You have to be extra careful not to hurt their feelings. They take everything personally, and instead of lashing out, they retreat, making you feel sorry for them.

Core-of-Hurters often feel unloved, un-special, unprotected and unworthy. They won't attempt to stop you from succeeding, but they won't help you to succeed either. They normally won't encourage you at all.

If you are not careful, you'll spend more time trying to encourage core-of-hurters to do things to help or improve themselves than you spend trying to improve yourself. Don't get caught up in this relationship. Your life will be at a standstill.

How to Deal with a Core-of-Hurt Personality

- Understand that just because they act hurt doesn't mean that you're hurting them.
- Don't get trapped in their moods or take responsibility for cheering them up.
- Remember, it is not in your power to make them happy.
- Try to deal calmly and simply with them, without a lot of emotion.
- Let them know ahead of time what behaviors and attitudes you will expect of them, and what they can expect of you.

CORE-OF-HEALTH PERSONALITY

These are definitely the type of people that can help you. They are open-minded, confident, and independent. They also have a good sense of humor. They are the kind of people that are able to be on your side and committed to you for the rest of your life. They are loyal, honest and sincere.

They don't hold grudges and when they are hurt, they usually bounce back quickly without trying to even the score. Core-of-health personalities often will encourage you in every aspect of your life journey, if you treat them right. These are the people to turn to in times of need.

Unfortunately, most people you meet will have either a core-of-hate or a core-of-hurt personality. It is OK to associate with them, but don't get drawn into their core values and beliefs. If you handle them effectively, and know their core personality, you may be able to deal with them. Just remember, don't attempt to change their personalities. It would waste your time and effort.

PROCRASTINATION

Nearly everyone puts off until tomorrow what should be done today. Procrastination, or putting tasks off, ranks among the top three self-defeating behaviors.

REASONS FOR PROCRASTINATING

There are many reasons why we procrastinate: self-doubt, boredom, fear of failure, the feeling of being unready or unprepared and so on. When you keep putting off things that you need or want to do, your real obstacle might not be laziness, the lack of confidence or fear, but it might be loneliness.

When you have someone to encourage you, guide you and reassure you that what you want to do can be done, your confidence, common sense and stick-to-it determination will be reinforced, especially when you are in doubt of your ability to complete a task.

The key to overcoming procrastination is to enlist the help of your support group. That is why people have jogging buddies, study groups and business partners. It is also why groups like Alcoholics Anonymous require that you find a "sponsor" to help you to stay sober through difficult times.

Try to find someone who will encourage your efforts. Try a loving parent, grandparent, friend or teacher—someone who will say "good job" when you finally complete the task that you have been avoiding. Ask for help! Don't be stagnant.

GETTING ANGRY AND MAKING THINGS WORSE

You gain momentary relief when you get angry, but often, you regret what you have done later. Not dealing with your anger is equally dangerous, because the feeling will fester and perhaps lead to depression and other medical problems.

AN OPTION FOR DEFUSING YOUR ANGER

You can convert your anger to what you believe in and respond on the basis of your belief. Once you see what has caused your anger, then you can develop the clarity, courage and strength to tell other why you feel the way you do, without exploding in rage.

Once you understand what and who caused your anger, then you can approach that individual and tell him or her why you feel violated and what you would like them to do to help you in resolving this conflict.

Whether dealing with offensive friends, a stubborn girl friend or a brazen bully, you can defuse your anger by explaining your beliefs and asking for help in resolving the conflict.

Here's how:

- Cool off. Resist the urge to act impulsively. Think over the situation.
- Ask yourself what made you angry—usually something you regard as unfair or unreasonable.
- Identify the beliefs that are being violated and write down how you can resolve this conflict.
- Ask for help from the one who violated your beliefs and from others to resolve the conflict.

LEARN FROM YOUR MISTAKES

If you are alive, you are going to make some mistakes. Human error is everywhere, and you are not by yourself when this happens to you. Making mistakes is not the problem. The problem is failing to admit that you made a mistake. Once you admit your mistake, you must learn from what you did wrong.

HOW TO AVOID SIMILAR MISTAKES

Expect that you learn from a mistake will help you to avoid a similar situation in the future. You should learn how to handle each mistake differently. Deciding not to let it happen again is a way to spare yourself the pain of figuring out what you did wrong. Again!

It is easy enough to mentally beat up on yourself or have others criticize you for your mistake—and this is going to happen. Try to limit this type of mental and verbal abuse by admitting that you made a mistake and then, if it's a big mistake, apologize for the mistake you made; then you move on. "Move on" doesn't mean forgetting what you did. It means trying to understand what you did wrong and making plans to handle the situation better the next time. THEN move on. Here's how:

- When you make a mistake, don't try to change it for at least 48 hours. Give what you did some time to sink in.
- Hate the mistake you made and not yourself for making the mistake.
- Review what you did wrong and think about what you would do if you could do things again.

REBELLING

You are at a stage in your life when you are learning a lot of things, especially grown up things. In a sense, you are growing up and moving into adulthood. It is quite natural for you to want to do things the way you want to do them. You are not alone.

DON'T TREAT ME LIKE A CHILD!

The problem is not that you are rebellious because you don't want to do what is being asked of you; it is that you don't want to do it, period. Being forced or coerced threatens your self-respect and compromises your dignity. It also makes you feel like a child.

As you mature, you will developed a certain amount of independence or free will. When this free will is threatened, doing what is right becomes less important to you than asserting your independence. Also, the outcome of your choice seems less important than making sure the choice is your own.

That's OK. Nothing is wrong with that. You are human. You are growing up. Sometimes, that independent spirit pays off. But remember, you may make additional mistakes in the learning process, if you decide to do things completely on your own and without input from others.

The key is that you should be choosing your actions, not merely going along to satisfy someone else. When you find yourself rejecting the wishes of others, make sure you are not rejecting your own wishes as well. Try to have a clear and well reasoned alternative in mind to others' wishes.

WANTING WHAT OTHERS HAVE

Grow up! You are not a kid anymore. You can't have everything that you want, unless you get it for yourself. Maybe I should rephrase this. You can have anything you want, if you obtain it with your own money or efforts. It is truly self-defeating to envy others success, status, clothes, car, good looks, etc.

BE HAPPY FOR OTHERS SUCCESS

You can feel good about what others obtain and you can make plans to duplicate what they have accomplished with hard work and dedication. Taking what others own is stealing and you know the consequences of that self-defeating behavior.

Also, thinking a lot about what other people have and what you don't have, could make you think of yourself as unworthy. This low opinion of yourself could discourage you from doing what is necessary for you to match the accomplishments of the person that you envy. Strangely, one way to deal with envy is to be around the people you envy. This is because your association with these people, if positive, may show you how to obtain the things that you want.

You may also learn that they had to endure challenges and hardships beyond anything you have experienced to get what they want. By associating with the people you envy, you will get to see that everything is not necessarily perfect in these people's lives.

ENVY CAN HELP YOU

Envy is good, if you handle it correctly. It can be the driving force to motivate you. You can begin to find ways to improve your abilities to help you obtain those things that you want.

Don't bother envying people who were born wealthy or with good looks. Just accept the fact that your fate and biology didn't give you these particular things and move on.

When you want what other people have, then you have set a goal for your life to help you obtain what others have. You have two choices to get what other people have. You can take it (steal it) from them or you can find out how they obtained what they have and take measures to duplicate their efforts to get what you want. That way you can begin to say to yourself, "I can do that too" instead of "I wish I had that."

Before you can use envy as a positive tool to help you to obtain those things that you want, you must first defuse any animosity you may feel towards others because they have what you want. Turn the animosity into admiration. Admire them for their success. Then turn admiration into emulation. By developing the same qualities that made them enviable, you can feel pride and deal with envy at the same time. Here are some tips:

- Try to appreciate and admire the person you envy.
- Find out what qualities or skills enabled that person to attain what you envy.
- Decide how you can duplicate those qualities and skills and make them your own.

HOLDING IT ALL IN

One source of anger, feeling down all the time and feeling unworthy is keeping a bad experience or a life-changing event to yourself. If you don't talk about an event, negative and positive, that has affected you, the impact of pain, fear and loss can cause all the above problems plus the feelings of loneliness.

SHARE YOUR PAIN

After you experience something bad in your life, a bad event, a bad person, loss of a life, a job, material objects, and so on, you need to talk about it to a friend, a parent, a mentor or a professional. Expressing yourself by telling your story is an important way of getting rid of all your pent-up feelings and emotions.

Talking it out eases the sense of isolation from others. By sharing your pain with others, you also find out that you are not alone. You'll find that others have had the same or similar experience, and they can relate to your experience and perhaps give you some insight to help you through your situation.

If you sit around holding on to tragic or dramatic life experiences, they can affect your mind, body and soul with potentially disastrous consequences.

Let this stuff go quickly by talking about it. This will begin to bring you relief and also faster and easier healing. Find a good listener with whom you can share your story. Don't hold on to this stuff. Think about it, talk about it and move on. Remember: in life, you will have pain. Deal with it.

QUITTING TOO SOON

When we start something, a business, a new job or a new relationship you get excited. The novelty and the freshness of a new idea or relationship excite you, but as reality sets in, and you realize that your new idea or relationship requires work-revising, fine-tuning and getting the bugs out- the thrill lessens, and you quit.

WHY WE QUIT TOO SOON

When something turns out to be more difficult than you anticipated, you are tempted to quit because you decide it is not worth the effort. Boredom is also another reason for quitting. If you can't tolerate the tedious process of working on an idea or relationship, you are bound to lose patience and quit.

The fear of humiliation can often shatter our desire to continue pursuing an idea or goal. You may not admit this even to yourself, but it may be the reason you want to quit. Quitting serves a two-fold purpose: It relieves frustration and anxiety, and it keeps you from confronting a deeper fear that we don't have what it takes to succeed.

The comfort of quitting seems more attractive than the hard work needed to reach your goals. When we quit repeatedly, we lose credibility in the eyes of your family and friends, and eventually in your own eyes as well. No one respects a quitter.

By quitting, you will never learn the skills that you need to overcome obstacles and frustration. You need perseverance to survive in all aspects of your life. Quitting means giving up, abandoning ideas, relationships and goals. It may release you from the burden of responsibility, but it leaves you caught in the grips of failure. Stick-to-itiveness pays off. Don't quit too soon.

BASIC LIFE SKILLS TEST

Before proceeding to the next section of this manual, take this test to insure that you understand what you just read and discussed. Put a check mark beside your answer to each question.

1. If there is a problem, who is responsible for solving that problem?
   ( ) My mother is responsible.
   ( ) My father is responsible.
   ( ) I am responsible.
2. What is manhood?
   ( ) Being able to get what I want.
   ( ) Being popular with the ladies.
   ( ) Overcoming obstacles in my path to success.
3. Who determines what is right or wrong for you?
   ( ) My mother makes the determination.
   ( ) My friends make the determination.
   ( ) I make the determination.
4. How does self-defeating behavior work against you?
   ( ) It hurts my family.
   ( ) It causes me to lose my friends.
   ( ) It works against my best interest.
5. Self-defeating behavior occurs when you fail to:
   ( ) be happy.
   ( ) be popular.
   ( ) learn from the lessons of life.
6. To overcome self-defeating behavior you must:
   ( ) quit smoking.
   ( ) ask someone you trust for help.
   ( ) ignore the problem.
7. What is self-defeating behavior?
   ( ) running from the police.
   ( ) not doing well in school.
   ( ) acting without regard to long-term consequence and considering reasonable alternatives.
8. If you have a setback, it means:
   ( ) that you are a failure.
   ( ) that you quit trying to be successful.
   ( ) that you will have to try harder and that you will try not to repeat your mistake.

9. You can defeat self-defeating behavior by:
   ( ) giving up.
   ( ) blaming others for the circumstances in your life.
   ( ) taking responsibility for your own action.
10. You can choose the right people in your life by:
   ( ) going with the flow.
   ( ) joining a gang.
   ( ) determine the core values and beliefs of a person before getting in-
      volved with him or her.

Chapter Two

Self-Esteem Training

Self-esteem is a deep-seated confidence in oneself and one's abilities that allows a person to face and conquer life's challenges. People with high self-esteem have the confidence to succeed in school, in sports and in any endeavor, because they know that they are talented. They dare to dream and turn those dreams into realities because they know they can. They don't do alcohol and drugs because they love and value themselves too highly to be self-destructive.

A man with low self-esteem loses the race every time because he never leaves the starting gate. He does not have the confidence or the belief in his own abilities to even try. He feels stupid, incompetent, and unworthy.

Why? Because he is used to hearing that he is stupid, lazy or bad. Quite often, he may hear this from a parent when they are angry (probably because their own parents told them that they were stupid too). Even teachers sometimes will make this mistake.

If you continue to hear these types of negative comments about yourself, eventually internalized negative beliefs begin to formulate in your mind.

These powerful and destructive beliefs that we absorb from others at an early ages, results in a chronic lack of self-esteem.

You are the most important person in your life. You must believe in yourself and not be affected by what others think or say about you. In the reality of life, only God is your judge.

This lack of self-esteem becomes the main ingredient in a life of fear, failure, and self-hate. If no one believes in you, then you will have a very hard time believing in yourself. That's why it is important to be around people, especially adults, who show you unconditional love and acceptance, not denigration and humiliation.

While growing and maturing in this society, two things can directly affect your self-esteem and self image: Television and school. Let look at each:

TELEVISION

Our society is hooked on television. You spend an average of four hours a day looking at TV. It stands to reason that your self-image and understanding of the world are heavily influenced by television. You are bombarded with images of smart and successful people, but few if any are minority or of your culture.

The self-image that is often suggested by TV is that of hoods, crooks, hip cats and drug addicts, especially when showing urban minority males. With this type of information continuously confronting you, eventually, you will begin to think that all urban men are dumb, unattractive and inferior to others.

SCHOOL

Our schools and colleges are an important part of our community. There are some impediments to the efforts our schools and colleges are making to educate a well-rounded student. They include poor funding, dilapidated buildings, outdated books and computers, classroom overcrowding, and crime.

The burdens of these problems are often felt by teachers who can become overwhelmed and sometimes hopeless. They, in turn, may take this frustration out on over active kids, mostly boys. They have little patience with the nonsense that these boys may carry-on in their classrooms.

Then too, our educational staffs are overwhelming female. Teachers, counselors, principals, parole officers and other key positions are typically women. Quite often, as human nature would have, males who act in an aggressive, anti-establishment and negative way are not what the average teacher wants to confront on the job, if the same problem exists in their personal life at home.

Hence, some teachers may lose control in these confrontations and in various ways, tell these bad kids that they have little ability or little chance of succeeding in school. Then too, you may be assigned to an educational program that does not encourage academic excellence, but it is only in place to get you out of the way of the successful students who want to learn. This could be or may already be devastating to you and your self-esteem, but we can't blame the teacher because in most cases, their reaction, whether positive or negative, was caused by your self-defeating actions.

The most important factor is your behavior in an educational facility. Your role is to do your work as well as you can and to cooperate with your teachers, principals, and the school staff. Remember, they are being paid to help you and they are the good guys!

SELF-ESTEEM AND LEARNING

The problem of low self-esteem is aggravated by overexposure, at an early age, to highly influential media in which the successful people you see are usually athletes, musicians, and rappers, not scientists or educators. When it comes to academics and learning, you have few good role models featured in the media on a daily basis.

You must develop the ability to observe successful role models. If these role models are smart and they achieve excellence in their career or profession, you will emulate their behavior and focus on doing the same.

The problem is that you are usually exposed to more non-intellectual models than to intellectual ones. So you don't see or know the other side of being successful. The result is that you have developed a stronger desire to be an athlete or a rapper because that is the only successful role model that you have been exposed to.

Some of our greatest athletes were pushed into and through college (many didn't graduate). They excel in sports, but they fail in their educational requirements. Many are suspended from school and lose full scholarships because they fail to understand the importance of an education.

Yet the irony is that these same athletes often have to be intelligent enough to study playbooks and play strategies. The intellect is there, but rarely guided from sports into other areas.

The same holds true for rap music artists. They know music and rhyme. This requires language skills and the ability to combine music with words. If you can accomplish great things with music and poetry (the rapping part), with some educational assistance, you probably can write a book.

Emulating rappers—shows that you have the intelligence to memorize an incredible amount of information with little effort, even though you probably didn't experience this drive or confidence to learn in school. If you can do this, as a rapper, you should have the confidence to learn math, English and other challenging subjects.

There is a saying, "A mind is a terrible thing to waste." This is true. You have a mind. It is yours to do with it as you please.

Those people who are successful as athletes and rappers were meant to be just what they are. They made an effort to expand that desire into learning everything they could about their chosen profession. You'll have to do the same. Your first step is to choose a career or profession and then make it your passion.

WHAT OTHERS THINK OF ME

At this time in your life, you may not realize it, but you are going through a stage. This stage of life, part of your Rites of Passage, is your rebellion stage.

This stage in life is a transition between your childhood and adult life. Here are some characteristics of this passage:

Anger: You seem to have a chip on your shoulder and you are aggravated by adult intervention into your life.

Rebellion: You are not open to agree with adults' comments and suggestions.

Attitude: You have an attitude about most things in your life, mostly a bad attitude.

Experimenting: You are experimenting with some things that are good and some that are bad.

Freedom: You are experiencing a new freedom. You have freedom of expression, of movement and you are free to make decisions on your own.

If you are experiencing any of these things, welcome to "The Rites of Passage." You are moving rapidly through a phase of your life that will be a blur in your later life. At this time it is can have a positive or negative affect on your present life and on your future events life.

As a teen and young adult, you are struggling to understand who you are and who you want to be. It is a tough struggle, and as you go through this transition, we adults have to contend with your behavior. Sometimes this behavior can be anywhere from extreme to outrageous.

The effect that your behavior can have on your family and friends, if it is negative, can last for many years. Forgiving and forgetting what you have done is hard for most people. Some of the things that you do (or say) during this transition from childhood to adulthood can leave long-lasting positive or negative feelings with family members and friends.

During this transition period, you have to be careful not to upset the balance of good feelings coming from family members and friends who are making a positive impact on your life. There is an old saying, "Don't bite the hand of the one who feeds you." Yes, it is just that serious. The most important part of your transition is how you come out of it when it is over and you become an adult.

Do you still have family members, friends and love ones who are committed to helping you in a positive way? Have you said things that alienated any

of your support group? (People who are helping you to survive by providing food, clothing and a roof over your head, an education, and financial help). If so, you need to start working to mend those bridges.

During your transition to adulthood, don't burn bridges with your support group. You will need their help as you move into adulthood and maybe for the rest of your life.

Many teens and young adults do not make it through "the Rites of Passage" without serious behavior problems. Ultimately, they run afoul of authority and the law, and they end up with criminal records that mark them for the rest of their lives. This will put them on the road to failure. These people are on a foolish and self-destructive road.

Two major factors often contribute to rebellion and getting into trouble. They are peer pressure and the media.

PEER PRESSURE

Peer pressure, or changing your beliefs to fit in with others, is perhaps one of the most powerful influences that you will face on a day-to-day basis. Your behavior is often governed by a need to fit in with the crowd. You want to be accepted as being hip or cool. This can often turn into behaving or even dressing like the group. This does not allow for much individuality or independent thinking.

The problem begins when the peer group is composed of others who have psychological and family problems. This may cause you to rebel and get in trouble with the law.

If you are a decent kid, you may not want to participate in destructive life activities, but you want to be accepted by your friends. In order for you to remain in the group, you are caught up in doing what everyone else does. If this is the case, you are lacking in self-esteem and you are susceptible to negative peer influences due to the lack of inner strength, confidence and independent thinking. In other words, finds some new friends who are doing positive things that you like to do.

Break the bond with people who later in life may end up on drugs, in jail or dead due to this early life involvement with self-destructive life activities.

THE MEDIA

The media: television, movies, recorded music, and other forms of media glorify the "gangsta" identity and the "thug" lifestyle in videos and CD's. You see so much of this from early childhood through adulthood that you may think that this stuff is a successful lifestyle. Don't be fooled.

Remember, the media are out to make money from these images that TV and music portray. They advertise and sell product on many of these negative programs that you watch. Many of these programs encourage you to be rebellious. This lifestyle is not really what you need during your "Rites of Passage" transition.

The media should encourage "freedom of thought and responsibility" because that is what you need at this time, but portraying a positive lifestyle in most instances, will not sell the products that they want you to buy. A positive lifestyle to many of your peers (and maybe you) is not cool. It's all about money. You be the judge.

What you watch on TV, the music you listen to on the radio and the products that you buy in the stores are all a part of the media hype. You may not realize what the media is doing to your mind until you come to the point in your life when the "gangsta lifestyle" has brought you to your knees. Then you will say—and it may be too late—"What hit me?"

LET'S DO SEX

Let's be real. Teenage pregnancies and sexually transmitted diseases are on the rise in urban communities. To think that you will refrain from premarital sexual activity and even to expect that you will use contraceptives before you participate in this type of activity is crazy, both on my part and that of our

moral society. Let's face it: sex is part of life, a very important part of life. Neither you nor I would be here if it weren't for sex. So what can we (as parents) say?

Well, we can hope that you will wait until you are married, but the probability of this happening is little or none. You are not alone. According to the Commission on Adolescent Sexual Health, three quarters of boys and half of the girls aged fifteen to nineteen have engaged in sexual intercourse. The numbers are probably greater for sex play or heavy petting.

We can ask you to refrain from sexual intercourse until after you are married and we can give you legitimate reasons why you should wait but this still may not convince you. We can also encourage you to join groups of young people who have decided to refrain from sexual intercourse until they marry. But extreme peer pressure, from girls (and sometimes grown women) who are attracted to you and who will encourage you to have sexual relations with them will put additional pressure on you. Also, sex on TV, videos and movies won't help. Your exposure to sex in everyday life will readily offset any gains that we would make. So what should we do?

We can try to scare you and make you think twice about the partners that you choose. HIV-AIDS has reached epidemic proportions among urban teens and that according to the Centers for Disease Control and Prevention, urban teenagers between the age of thirteen and twenty-four account for sixty-three percent of all new HIV infections.

You are probably thinking, "Well, this won't happen to me!" Again, if you thinking this way, you are not by yourself. According to a recent study on AIDS, despite continual education and warnings, nearly nine out of ten youth still remain skeptical (or don't believe at all) that they can get HIV from sex. Statistically, as you can see, you have a pretty good chance of getting a disease that will affect you and your ability to have sex for the rest of your life. Is it worth it? You tell me.

So What Can You Do?

This high rate of sexually transmitted diseases, as well as teen pregnancies, is directly due to a lack of to-the-point sexual education, that is, sexual education that is telling you exactly how things are. Sexual ignorance results in some very unhealthy practices and behavior. You are facing the following issues:

Unprotected Sex is Still Rampant

Do you still think that you can't get HIV from having sex? Do you still think that this only happens to drug abusers and alternative lifestyle people?

Are You Having Risky Sex?

If you are having a lot of sex, beware. If you break the foreskin on your penis, and there is bleeding, HIV infected blood transmitted to an open wound is one of the primary causes of HIV infection.

Are You Using Condoms Correctly?

So if we can't convince you to abstain from sex, the availability and social acceptance of condoms has promoted safer sex. Are you using condoms? Are you using them right?

Are You Using the Wrong Condom?

Do you use a lambskin condom? These condoms can actually allow venereal diseases to come through. Also, if you reuse a condom, it will break. Condoms that break often cause sexually transmitted diseases or pregnancies.

Do You Have a lot of Sexual Partners?

You are really looking for problems. If you are skipping school to have sex or group sex, you are probably mixing drugs and alcohol to make your party better. Well, the use of these chemicals usually will result in your being unable to make a good judgment about sex partners and safe sex. Consider this also, if she is having sex with multiple men in group sex, just think what type of disease she might have gotten during her sexual encounters with those guys before you.

Unprotected sex is like playing Russian roulette. Your chances of catching a deadly sexually transmitted disease are increased by the number of sexual encounters that you have. Numerous sexual encounters will increase the probability of getting a sexually transmitted disease.

Take precautions and think before you leap. Better still, don't leap . . . Abstain!

BABIES

Each year there are nearly 900 thousand teen pregnancies in the United States. Eight in ten of these pregnancies are unintended and seventy-nine percent are to unmarried teens.

Fact

- Thirteen percent of all babies born in the U.S. are born to teens. For every sexual encounter that you have, you have a better then 1 in 10 chance of producing a baby.
- Twenty-five percent of teenage mothers have a second child within two years of their first. If she already has a baby, there is a 1 in 4 chance that a sexual encounter with her will produce another baby.

Think about this. The cost of child support for your child that you may be required to pay is from $54,000 to $108,000 on average over an eighteen-year period. This money comes out of your income. This is in addition to the other costs of bringing up a child for more than eighteen years. You can believe me when I tell you that this won't end at eighteen.

Think of this too, you will have to pay $250 to $350 or more every month for child support from your income to take care of your kid or you could end up in jail if you don't pay. Sure, this is your kid, you say, but look what else your kid may be facing your child over his or her lifetime.

Fact

For teenage parents and their children, the prospects for a healthy and productive life are significantly reduced. The infants and children of teenage mothers also face greater health and developmental risks; they have lower birth weights; they are more likely to perform poorly in school; they are at greater risk of abuse and neglect; and they are more likely to be involved in the criminal justice system.

And what about you, the father?

Fact

Teenage fathers complete less education (you are too busy working to pay child support) and earn less than men who wait to have children later in life. Adolescent dads will finish an average of only 11.3 years of school by age 27, compared to nearly 13 years by their counterparts who delayed fathering a child until age 21.

By age twenty-seven, adolescent fathers earn less annually than a comparison group of men who delay fathering until age twenty or twenty-one. Fathering a child will put your career and life on hold. Are you prepared to accept this responsibility?

MARRIAGE

You want to get married? Don't even think about it. If you are under twenty-five years of age, marriage is a BIG responsibility and most guys your age are not quite ready for it.

Fact

Most teen mothers have expectations for marrying the father of their child, however, not even eight percent of unwed mothers are married to the baby's father within one year of giving birth.

Fact

Teenage marriages are unstable; one-third of teenage marriages formed before the bride is eighteen years old end in divorce within five years, and almost half end within ten years.

Fact

Teen mothers, fathers, and their children are vulnerable to severe adverse social and economic consequences. Many of the children live in poverty during their most critically important developmental years.

Children of teen parents spend years trying to catch up educationally and economically, and they are more likely to be involved with the child welfare system.

Fact

Research suggests that children do best with two parents who have a healthy marriage.

Teens who are determined to marry should seek out and obtain marriage education, job training, and family planning services (to prevent subsequent births too soon).

I am not promoting teen marriage, because research has shown that few teen marriages are long lasting and increase child well being. However, for the few teen marriages, additional support services may help to increase the likelihood of a healthy outcome for their children.

Marriage—to be specific: don't even think about it!

GANGS

Violent street gangs are active in almost all medium size, as well as large, urban cities in America. Growing to manhood is a time of estrangement from your parents (you don't want to be around them). Since gangs appeal to youth who need a "family," you are vulnerable to all aspects of gang membership.

There are a number of reasons why gang membership is attractive to urban youth. Youth with low self-esteem are always at risk for antisocial behavior. They often try to compensate and falsely build up self-esteem by breaking the rules of acceptable behavior.

It is easier for you, if you have low self-esteem, to join the wrong crowd, such as a gang, because membership brings you emotional and physical security. Gangs are admired and feared. They are seen as the top dogs on the streets and in schools. They rule by numbers, fear and intimidation. On the downside, however, gangs can get you into jail, physically harmed or killed.

As you move into adulthood, you will see that not all gangs are bad; some are positive. In college, fraternities and clubs are like gangs, but those non-violent groups are formed for some of the same reasons. Clubs are a form of gang. These are non-violent groups that are formed for the same reasons as gangs are. Like-minded people, looking to identify with people of similar beliefs, goals and persuasions, form them

It's not necessary to join a negative group because there are plenty positive groups you can join that will give you some of the same satisfaction as being in a gang. In such groups there is also less risk of the negative impacts of a gang membership such as physical harm and/or death.

PRISON AND JAIL

A surprisingly large number of urban youth populate our jails and prisons. There are over one million minority males currently in jail according to the U.S. Department of Justice statistics with another 978,000 on probation.

Nationwide, an average of thirty percent of our urban young adult population is in jail, on parole or in the justice system. This is a national disgrace. In some urban cities as high as fifty percent of our urban youth are involved in some way with jail, probation or the criminal justice system.

As an urban youth, you have a 1 chance in 6 of ending up in jail before you are thirty years of age. This means that one in every six urban youth will end up in jail in his lifetime. Right now, one in every three urban youth will end up in some form of problem with the law.

THE POLICE AND YOU

What does dealing with the police have to do with your self-esteem? If you are assertive, remember that when you deal with the police, assertive behavior is interpreted as a challenge and a threat to police authority, and this misunderstanding can often trigger aggressive police behavior.

In other words, if the police confront you, and you are not properly prepared to deal with a police confrontation, you won't stand a chance against the brute force of THE POLICE.

Don't even think about it! You don't have a chance! Even if you are not caught right away for some criminal act, you will never be able to relax and be sure that your life is safe.

If you do something today that is illegal, forensic evidence detection tools and DNA identification capabilities will convict you. There is little or no chance of your escaping from THE POLICE. So, you've got to decide to prevent a potentially dangerous situation and avoid criminal activity.

Understand this: you can't win in criminal activity. Eventually, you will get caught or someone will turn you in.

Here are some rules of conduct for dealing with the police:

1. Don't get into a situation that will necessitate police intervention. Stay away from friends and groups that desire to challenge the police.
2. Remember, the police exist to protect the community and you. They do not exist just to arrest urban youth.
3. Remember, you can't win if you provoke or anger a police officer. There are charges above and beyond what you know that can be placed on you that will put you in jail.
4. Never run from the police, especially after you have been told to stop and not to move.
5. Do not make any sudden moves or gestures in the presence of police, even if they are not paying attention to you. The police are trained to react to sudden gestures and movements as a threat to their physical person and you can be physically hurt or shot.
6. If you are placed under arrest, do not fight or resist the police. They will become angrier, resulting in a physically violent or deadly response.
7. Always address a police officer with respect. In most instances they will treat you the same way that you treat them. Always respond in an appropriate manner that will not challenge the officer's authority.
8. Stay calm. Don't talk too much. Do not make any confessions. Commit to memory everything that has happened during your encounter with the police. Ask them to call your parents or school.

SUMMARY

Young urban adult males have a tough road in American society. The truth is that you will continue to be confronted with racism and prejudice because you are who you are. Get over it. It exists. There is nothing you can do to change it. It will always exist because it is a fixture in life.

You can sit around and get upset or depressed about racism and prejudice, but that's not going to help your individual situation. Remember during this transition into manhood, you have got to help yourself before you can solve the problems of the world. You cannot change what is happening in the world until you change yourself.

Yes, there is raw and scientific racism. There are media stereotypes, anti-affirmative action programs, institutional racism, and more. So what!

Racism and prejudice have been a part of this society (and many others) long before you were born and will continue long after you are gone. What is important now, as you reach this turning point in your life is—is how you will respond to racism and prejudice!

Run, hide, fight, protest, give up, or rebel? These are some of your options. The biggest challenge you have as an urban youth dealing with racism and prejudice is to keep them from affecting your spirit. You don't want to let this damage your self-image and lower your self-esteem.

If you shut down and accept the brainwashing that you hear, see, and experience—such as minorities being inferior on TV, in the movies, and in other media—you will have problems making your transition to manhood. If you accept the beliefs that all urban youth like gangster rap music, fail in school, don't go to college, live in ghettos, usually don't get good jobs, usually fail, speak gangster talk, shuck and jive, are the best athletes, and so on, you will fail.

Yes, racism, discrimination and prejudice hurt your psyche, but only if you let them. The wrong response to these obstacles can cause you to miss educational and professional opportunities. Your mind, your thoughts and your attitude must be conditioned to overcome everything that comes into the way of your success in life.

You need to understand that the bad things you expect to happen to you will happen. Your mind is just that strong. If you think something will prevent you from succeeding, it will.

You must work hard to defeat the racism, discrimination and prejudice you meet. You can use racism and prejudice as fuel to drive yourself to succeed in spite of them. But if you decide that life is a dead-end proposition, that decision will lead you to drugs, gang activity, other self-destructive behavior, and even death.

I WANT TO LIVE

Stop feeling sorry for the little old minority kid who grew up in poverty—the ghetto—, who didn't have much to eat or clothes to wear, no father—sometimes no mother—, who got on drugs, got locked up, failed school, couldn't find a job, who was discriminated against, stereotyped as stupid, lazy, incompetent and always failing at everything he did and so on. This story is old. Some of the most successful urban adults rose beyond these obstacles and succeeded. You can too.

Let's look at such great people as Martin Luther King, Malcolm X and General Colin Powell, the first African American five-star general of the armed forces (not the army, not the navy, not the marines, nor the air force . . . but over the entire U.S.A. Armed Forces).

They had backgrounds and obstacles similar to yours, but they overcame all their obstacles and succeeded beyond their greatest expectations. Read a book on their life stories and see for yourself.

All of our urban minority greats soared to great heights because their personal goal was to succeed by smashing the barriers of racism and establishing equality, first for themselves and then for others.

You too can succeed by letting the obstacles of racism and prejudice fuel your drive to overcome the odds against you and the stumbling blocks in your way. So you grew up poor! It didn't stop General Colin Powell. So you got locked up! It didn't stop Don King, the millionaire-boxing promoter.

Start reading the life stories of our great leaders. You'll see that your life may be similar to theirs, and that they did not let adversity stop them. They let adversity push them to success, against all odds. You can do this too.

SELF-ESTEEM TRAINING TEST

Before proceeding to the next section of this manual, take this test to ensure that you understand what you have just read and discussed.

1. What is self-esteem?
   ( ) Feeling good about my friend.
   ( ) A deep-seated confidence in my abilities and myself.
   ( ) Being able to talk to people.
2. What does self-esteem help me to do?
   ( ) It allows me to meet more successful people.
   ( ) It allows me to face and conquer life's challenges.
   ( ) It gives me the confidence to succeed in school, sports, and in any endeavor.
   ( ) All of the above.
3. Who is the most important person in my life?
   ( ) My football coach.
   ( ) My mother.
   ( ) I am the most important person in my life.
4. Why is TV bad for my self-esteem?
   ( ) It is boring.
   ( ) It displays a negative image of who I am.
   ( ) It has too many commercials.
5. Teachers are:
   ( ) paid to help me to be successful.
   ( ) paid to always be on my case.
   ( ) paid to stop me from having fun.
6. If I am successful playing sports, I should be intelligent enough to:
   ( ) be a good basketball player.
   ( ) run faster than my friends.
   ( ) do well and succeed in school.
7. What is the most important part of my transition from teenager to manhood?
   ( ) That I still have positive and committed family members.
   ( ) That I do good in school.
   ( ) That I make the NBA.
8. How am I going to deal with sex?
   ( ) Understand its use and purpose.
   ( ) Realize that it can cause pregnancies or sexually transmitted diseases.
   ( ) Try to abstain until after marriage.

( ) All of the above.

9. Should I get married before twenty-one years of age?

( ) Yes, I am prepared to take on the responsibility of taking care of a wife and child.

( ) Yes, I am in love.

( ) No. I should not think about it until then, or even later.

10. Gangs are good:

( ) if the gang is made up of people with good moral beliefs and values.

( ) if I am safe from any physical or mental harm.

( ) if the group was formed to do positive tasks and deeds.

( ) All of the above.

Chapter Three

Finding My Career and Life Purpose

WHAT LIFE IS ALL ABOUT

Your life is based as much on failure as on success. Success, failure and adversity form the rungs of a ladder that all men have to climb to get to a good and useful life.

So it is with you. In you life passage from adolescence to adulthood you will find that, with luck, the wreckage of past failures forms a road map on which the lessons from your failures will help you to move forward in the future. Sometime you will fail at something, and you will remember that failure, but most of the time, this too shall pass. Other time, you'll forget failures and, in most instances, you will fail again with the same type of failure because you didn't study your past failure and learn from it.

Failing is good. Failure prepares you for success, if you learn from that failure. The map of experience is just like a road map. You use the map of suc-

cesses and failures to bring you to your ultimate goal. That goal is to help others to learn what you have learned and to help them to succeed. That's what life is all about. Without failure, you cannot make this transition.

Some people handle failure as if it just part of life, and some handle failure as the ultimate fall-the end. Which person are you? You must now understand, as you move from a young adult stage to manhood that life must go on.

You must get up everyday and go out and participate in this game called life. It is like playing football or basketball. Some days are tougher then other days, but you still go on. Some days you are a winner and some days you are a loser. When things go wrong, just look forward to a new day when you can get up and go start all over again.

Boring? Not really. The key to your success in life is not in hoping to reach big goals and successes overnight. Life only allows you to succeed one-small-step-at-a-time. If you think that you can rush success, well, good luck. Many have tried and most have failed.

Little steps. That is what life allows. The key to getting through each little step to your ultimate success is getting up each day and showing up to participate in this game of life. When you take these little steps, sometimes you can take bigger steps and sometimes you will fall flat on your face.

Remember, you have to be in the game in order for something to happen. With each step, you get closer to the goal that you set for yourself. If you are not participating in the game, you won't win.

Forget about quitting. Who cares that you are poor, uneducated, a high school dropout and that you had problems with substance abuse. Set all this aside. Stop. Think. Make a decision right now. Start playing the game of life?

Showing up for life everyday is the most important part of surviving. Just show up. That is THE game. Think of life as your movie. You write the script. You decide who will win and who will lose. You decide who becomes a success,

who will be rich or who will end up downtrodden and broke. Showing up every day for life gets you to continue your struggle—and it is a struggle—to achieve what you have set in your mind on achieving.

It's on you. No matter what obstacles may come up to stop you, you must pick yourself up, go at it again, and continue in this game. You have to STOP, THINK, and make a decision as to which way to turn when obstacles and problems confront you.

Running away only prolongs your frustration and that leads to the loss of hope and to failure. You must choose among many choices to solve your problems. You alone are responsible for the solution.

In the game of life, you are not competing with or against other people. You are really playing against yourself. Your frustrations and fears are your only shortcomings. If you can get past these two things, then you are on your way to success. It's a mind thing. In life, you are competing against your mind-the positive side and the negative side.

I was told many years ago by elders—and I didn't want to listen then—that whatever you want or dream of having in life, if you believe it, you can achieve it. This only let's you know that your mind is very powerful—even a high school dropouts mind. In the game of life you are competing against yourself to achieve your dreams or not to achieve your dream

It is a constant battle with obstacle like fear and negative thoughts, with failures, thrown in the way to complicate matters. At the same time, you are fighting your inner self to stay on target. Such is life. To stay on target, you need to take small steps towards your dream. These small steps are called setting goals.

SETTING GOALS

Surviving the day-to-day mess of life is hard in itself. The first goal that you should set is to keep the hard, tough days from taking you out of this game of life. The next important thing to remember is that our ultimate goal or dream is the most important part of our life.

golden
parachute

The value of the race lies in reaching the finish line. You must remember that the finish line and the way to reach the finish line is by taking small steps. Each step takes you closer to the goal in front of you. It is the attention that you pay to each step that will lead you to your goals. Small steps are goals too. Without goals, there wouldn't be any successes. If you focus your energies on the small steps leading to your goals, you will reach each small goal and ultimately, the big dream.

SO YOU WANT TO BE RICH

Since the author is nowhere near rich, he can only quote some of the things that he has been told through the years that might help you to reach this goal. First and foremost, you have to start somewhere before you get rich. You have to earn money before you can make more money. So start out slowly.

Start with a goal to pay your own way. Rent your own apartment, buy your own groceries, buy a car, and so on. Take these small steps first because they will lead you to even larger goals and accomplishments. Your first goal should be self-sufficiency. You should strive to take care of yourself. Pay your own bills, own your own car and live in your own place. Of course, you will need to start your own business or get a good paying job to accomplish these things. To get the knowledge to start your own business or to get a good paying job, you will need a good education. Getting an education or learning a business or trade is the key to starting a successful business or getting a good paying job. Without some education, you can still become rich, but you will have to work a little longer and harder to reach the top. But you can if you turn desire into money. Working gives you a reason to live and it helps you to reach your goals. You've got to start somewhere. Start a business or get a job first.

We are living at the greatest time in all human history. More people are becoming wealthy today (starting from nothing) than ever before imagined. Here is the best news of all. Virtually everyone started with nothing. More than ninety percent of all rich people started off broke or nearly broke. The average self-made millionaire has failed many times before becoming rich. And what hundreds of thousands of other people have done, you can too.

Most self-made millionaires are ordinary people just like you and I. They had average educations, worked average jobs and they lived in average neighborhoods. They stopped being average by using their brains. They found out what the financially successful people do and they did those same things over and over again until they achieved the same results.

In your search for wealth, remember that you must do specific things over and over again until you achieve your desired goals. I challenge and encourage you to research and find out what these things are. I know what they are, but this is a good subject for another workshop. GOOD LUCK with your life.

LIFE CHOICES

A good job and solid career can make life much more pleasant. With a good job, or your own business, you can pay your rent, buy groceries, stylish clothes, and a nice car. In time, you can even buy a house, get married, start a family and have all the good things of life. You have five (5) life choices that you can make to help you to get the things in life that you desire:

1. GET AN EDUCATION.
2. JOIN THE MILITARY.
3. GET A JOB.
4. START A BUSINESS.
5. BE A BUM.

It's that simple. There are no other choices. It is up to you to decide which direction to follow. You may choose one of the first four options and it might

not work for you. So go to the next option. Just stay away from # 5! Keep trying until an option—or multiple options—works for you.

Sometimes a combination of each option can lead to self-sufficiency. That's what it is all about: SELF—SUFFICIENCY . . . making it on your own.

With any of the first four options, you can make life much more pleasant. Again, if you have a good job, or your own business, you can pay your rent; buy groceries; a nice car and stylish clothes. In time, you can even buy a house, get married, start a family and have all the good things of life.

You may have to go to college, to a trade school or some other programs to develop skills to sell to others. To earn more money, you need specialized skills. It is ok to be a doctor, but a surgeon specializing in back surgery or eye surgery, gets paid more money. A producer or director of rap music CD's is paid more money then a rap artist. An owner of a football team makes more money then the football player/star, because he is the person paying the players salary. Specialized work skills and business skills pay more money.

You can join the military—the army, navy, marines, or air force—to obtain training and skills. The military has its risk, but the benefits that you receive will include discipline, free travel, free training, free health insurance, a place to live, a bonus for joining and in most instance, a free college education.

The primary purpose of each of the above life choices is to get skills that you can sell to others. Without skills to sell, you won't get very far or be very successful in life. Therefore, it is important to choose one of these four choices after high school. A skill is a must to survive in the game of life. Without skills you can be a bum.

FINDING WORK

A good job and a solid career can make life much more pleasant. With a good job, or your own business, you can have all the good things of life. I keep repeating this because this is important.

You may have to go to college, to a trade school or some other programs to develop skills that you can sell. Your skills are what you give to the world in exchange for money you use to purchase the things you need. You have to trade your services, your work and your skills for money.

The primary purpose of getting an education is to get skills that you can sell to others. Without skills to sell, you won't get very far or be very successful in life. Therefore, it is important to obtain an education after high school. A skill is a must to survive in the game of life.

You can be a good and honorable man, be of service to others, and make money at it. The amount of money you receive in exchange for the service that you give is a measure of the value of your service. We like to get paid for what we do, but you are paid more money based on the value of your service. Services provided by doctors and lawyers are highly valued and they bring more money because they are greatly needed by others.

Think about your skills and how they will affect your life when your schoolwork starts to get you down and when you find it hard to focus on your education. Remember that education is a necessary part of your life and it is necessary for you to obtain skills for services that you can offer for income.

If you are to succeed in life, you must study and learn skills that you can use to earn a living. With no skills, you cannot earn enough to accomplish the goals and reach the dreams that you may have.

You must strive to learn from the cradle to the grave. You must also realize that being school smart is not for sissies and weak men. With school smarts and street smarts, a young man has a step ahead of many young men who have just street smarts.

Your first goal should be to obtain an education.

FINDING A JOB

Finding a job is easy. You can look in the employment section of the Sunday newspaper. Go to the Internet. Type in the word "JOBS". There are numerous job websites that list many job categories, locations and places to send your resume'. Ask your friends if their employers are hiring new people. Decide what type of job you would like to do and go to businesses that have these jobs. Ask if they are hiring. Be proactive—ASK.

YOUR RÉSUMÉ

Getting the type of job that you want takes a lot of work. Remember, when one employer turns you down, there is someone else out there who is going to tell you "Yes". Advice: When you're turned down, DON'T TAKE IT PERSONAL!

Before you get a job interview, you have to convince the potential employer that you are a worthwhile candidate for the job that you want. Your résumé is the first impression the interviewer has of you. It needs to be top notch.

Don't send in something that is handwritten, dirty and full of errors. It may cost you a little money to do it professionally or get your mom or a friend to help you. It is well worth the extra effort.

Employers who look at a neat, carefully-written résumé, think, "This person knows how to present himself and has a professional attitude. I want to meet him". A well-written résumé makes you stand out from competitors who are trying to get the same job that you are trying to get. Believe me: there is a crowd going after the job you want. It is very important that you make a good impression before you meet your potential employer.

In most instances, your chances of getting an interview for a job will depend on how well your résumé is written; it's your first impression. Want to know how to write a great résumé? Go to the Internet or your public library to obtain this information. On the Internet, you can find books on how to write a résumé and actual guidelines for writing one.

My advice on writing a résumé is to keep it short and simple. Also, tell the truth. Your potential employer will check everything that you say about yourself. I advise you to leave out the unimportant negative info—a low high school grade point average or a juvenile misdemeanor. If it is not pertinent to the job, leave out the negative stuff.

THE JOB INTERVIEW

A job interview is just another type of business meeting. If you are inter-viewing for a full-time position, a temporary position, or a contract position, the following ideas and techniques will apply.

Once you have an appointment, the way you look and act are especially im-portant. To say that you have to be on your best behavior is right. The quick-est way to discredit yourself—and not get the job—is to be dressed or groomed inappropriately for a job interview.

Remember, studies show that most employers make up their mind about you within the first thirty seconds of meeting you. So leave the "GANSTA" look and attitude behind you when you enter that door. Acting that way may impress your friends, but it will turn off a potential employer IMMEDI-ATELY and you won't get the job.

FIRST IMPRESSIONS

Even if you are hired, your relationship with the interviewer will be influ-enced by his or her first impression of you. First impressions have more im-pact than performance, family, or all the time you've spent to be educated and trained in your skill or profession.

You must look your best for every job interview. You don't have to have a closet full of expensive clothing, but you need to look neat and professional.

If your clothes are too tight, your weight will be magnified and you will look unprofessional. If your hair needs combing, your whole appearance will suffer. If your beard or moustache needs trimming, you'll appear to be sloppy. If you have body odor, no amount of talent or skill will get people to hire you.

If you are a smoker or you live with a smoker, don't come to a job inter-view smelling like tobacco smoke. Numerous employers today strive to hire non-smokers, and you will be immediately disqualified if you show up with cigarette, cigar or even alcohol odor on your breath or clothing.

Advice: Don't bring your friends to the job interview. Your friends could eliminate your chances too.

YOUR SELF-CONFIDENCE IS IMPORTANT

Your self-confidence increases when you know that you look good and you are well groomed. If you look like a million dollars to yourself, the chances are that you'll look good to other people.

NONVERBAL INTERVIEWING TIPS

The following non-verbal tips will help prepare you for the interview process. Studies prove that ninety-three percent of how people judge you during an interview does not involve your words; it is nonverbal. Fifty-five percent is in your appearance, thirty-five percent is the tone of your voice, and three percent is your gestures. When you are interviewing for a job, try to use these nonverbal actions:

- Maintain eye contact.
- Sit on the front of your chair and lean forward.
- Use your head and face to agree with both positive and negative statements.
- Speak at a moderate rate, volume and pitch.
- Keep your hands in an open, unhidden position.
- Keep your legs, arms and feet uncrossed.
- Keep still—don't fidget, drum your fingers, or crack your knuckles.

HOW TO BEHAVE DURING AN INTERVIEW

1. Be prepared to talk about yourself with confidence. Be comfortable with the question, "Why should we hire you?" When the interviewer says, "Tell me about yourself," don't get scared and say "Uhhh" or "there's not much to tell." Interviewers often ask questions to determine how well

you can carry on a conversation. They want to determine whether you are sure of yourself, whether you are too confident or not confident enough.

Most employers want answers to these three questions: "Can this applicant do the job?" "Will this applicant do the job?" "Does this applicant fit the job?" Make sure you present your qualifications in these areas:

- Your ability and willingness to work. Stress your outstanding life accomplishments, skills, specific knowledge, ideas or concepts. Stress the good things about you that separate you from other applicants.
- Flexibility. Your ability and willingness to learn new ways of doing things is a highly valued qualification. If you are new to the business world, stress that you are willing to be trained.
- Communication skills. Next to job skills, communication skills—how you talk to others—is the most important attribute that you can offer an employer. That includes getting along with other people.
- Understanding the organization. Know the company and what they do before the interview. Then you will be able to let the interviewer know why hiring you can add to the company's success.
- Good health. Most interviewers want to know as much as possible about your mental and physical health. They are impressed by a person who looks fit and in control, and who seems relatively stress free.
- Tests. Most companies will test you-on the spot-to see if you do drugs. If you test is positive, move on to the next job interview because you blew your chances here. Some companies will even give you a test to determine your mental attitude and your physical condition. Don't panic. Just keep a positive attitude and do the best you can on the test. Remember, there is no better correlation between your characteristics and your health than a positive attitude.
- Honesty. Businesses want to hire employees who will not hurt or steal from the company. Don't take it personal. Past experiences with former employees makes the interviewer worry about hiring the wrong person. Since interviewers are limited in the kinds of questions that they can ask about your honesty, and you need to convince the interviewer that you are committed, have good integrity and that you have good personal values.

2. Be prepared for questions. You should already have the answers for the questions that the interviewer will ask you. Don't deliver a memorized

response, but practice the answers before you start going to interviews. The more you practice, the less frightening the questions will be. You should prepare yourself and be ready for the questions. Here are some of the most common questions that you can expect:

- Tell me about yourself.
- Why do you want this job?
- Where do you want to be in five years?
- What do you want from this job?
- What did you like most and least about your last job?
- How do you get along with other people?
- What was the most difficult situation that you faced in your last job?
- What are your three greatest strengths and weaknesses?
- Is there anything else that you would like to tell me?

3. Use discretion. Tell the interviewer about your strength. But if they come right out and ask what your greatest weakness is, tell them; and describe it in a way that shows you are managing it well. Don't be ashamed of it.

4. Be prepared with questions. When the interviewer asks if you have any questions for them, have some ready. Ask questions about the company, the industry, and the particular job. Discuss the major priorities you see in this job. Ask what you are expected to accomplish in the first year? Don't lead the interviewer to believe that all you care about is the money.

5. Use silence wisely. Silence is powerful in an interview, and most interviewers are good at using it. If you use silence to your benefit, and not just because you are afraid to answer a question, you will have a definite advantage. Unless you are asked to give more details, speak less than three minutes in response to any question.

6. Be especially careful about touch. When you are in an interview, shaking hands is the only way you should touch the interviewer. Use non-physical forms of touching such as eye contact before, during, and at the completion

of the interview. Pull your head up, make direct eye contact, smile, and tell them the information you've prepared.

7. Calling the interviewer by name. Another form of touch you can use safely is to call the interviewers by name. Repeat their names when you meet for the first time. Call them by name during the interview—but not excessively. Call them "Mr." or "Ms." when responding to them and use their names again when you leave. For example, "Mr. Jones, thank you for having me in for the interview; it was a pleasure meeting you."

8. Smile. It is important to smile, but don't over do it. Relax! Don't be afraid to laugh. Do it with dignity and don't over do it. Don't stress out during the interview. If you look relaxed and comfortable during the interview, the interviewer will know that you will be comfortable on the job. So relax and accept the interview as a challenge.

9. Don't smoke before, during and after the interview. Studies have shown that nonsmokers are much more likely to get and to hold the top jobs in companies. A nonsmoking interviewer can smell your smoke, no matter how long before the interview that you smoked.

10. Always send a thank you note after the interview. This may sound mushy, but interviewers who have interviewed hundreds of candidates for a job, are extremely impressed by the applicant who sends a simple reminder of who he is. If you do that, it may be enough to push you into the top job candidates' list. It might just get you the job. Give it try. You never know.

HOW TO BEHAVE AT WORK

Congratulations! You got the Job! You have just become the "new kid on the block". People will be watching you closely. Don't get stressed. Follow this basic guideline of work behavior and you'll do just fine:

BASIC GUIDELINES

1. Be careful with your appearance. Dress the way your company requires you to dress.
2. Honor other people's desk space and cubicles.
3. Expand your knowledge. Learn as much as you can about your job and your manager's job and how they fit into the overall company. Learning as much as you can, will help you to adapt better and teach you to be more flexible. You will also learn to deal with changes in your company and you will also learn how to expand your job.
4. Honor your working hours. Always be on time for work. As a rule, if you are going to be more then five minutes late, call your supervisor and let him or her know the reason. Don't spend company time eating at your desk, talking at the water fountain or making personal phone calls. Take a few minutes to clean yourself up as you prepare to leave your job, but only after your working hours are over.
5. Be friendly. When you are new, you need people to help you with your new duties and to explain the procedures. They also will need to show you where to get information or materials you'll need. Make an extra effort to get along with everyone. Don't try too hard and annoy someone who may not want to get along with you.

6. Keep personal information to yourself. When someone asks you how you are doing, don't tell him or her your life story and all your personal business. That person will tell someone else what you said and it will be all over the office. Some of this information could be used against you later. If you don't have anything else to say, just be quiet and go about your way. Don't discuss your salary or any other confidential or personal information about yourself or your coworkers. Just do your work and stay out of it.
7. Be positive and supportive.
8. Keep an open mind. Make informed judgments. Avoid jumping to conclusions. Don't be a party gossip. Think before you talk about any job subject or problem.
9. Follow through. Cover every angle of a project that you are required to do, and don't wait to be reminded that you need to finish the project. Be

realistic about how long a project should take. If you are not sure, ask your supervisor.

10. Communicate. Only job knowledge ranks above communication skills as a factor for workplace success. Everyone wants to know what is going on, primarily on a major work project. Your supervisors want you to go through the normal channels of communication on everything that happens on the job. Don't go over their heads and don't bring them things that don't concern the job. If you disagree with them, do it tactfully, with a positive alternative, and at a good time of the day.

11. Listen. Speaking and listening are twin skills. Both must occur in order to have good communication. You also learn more by listening to what others know. Listen to how others organize their ideas and how they respond to changes in procedures. Show that you want to learn. Establish yourself as someone who wants to get the job done right.

12. Solve your own problems. When you have a problem, bring possible solutions to the table. Don't complain about things that cannot be changed, and don't blame others when you make a mistake. Accept responsibility and work hard to insure that it doesn't happen again. Learn to accept criticism without being defensive.

13. Work hard. Be ready and willing to take on new responsibilities. Do more than expected. Don't be content to do only what you are required to do. Look for areas in which you can do more and make yourself more valuable.

14. Don't be in too big a hurry to advance. Learn as much as you can in the job you have now. Think ahead. No matter how good and eager you are, it takes time to move up on your job. There may be others who work with you who are moving up faster and getting a salary raise before you. Remember, you never know what their situation is. They may have more

education then you do in the field in which you are working or they may be the employer's family member who is in a training program to learn all facets of the business before moving into management. Be patient. Your promotion will come.

GOOD PERSON TO PERSON COMMUNICATION

1. Always make solid eye contact when you talk.
2. Display good posture.
3. Be relaxed and natural when you speak.
4. Dress and groom for the environment you are in.
5. Always talk in a rich and steady voice.
6. Use good clear language, no non-words or slang.
7. Listen closely to understand what others are trying to say.
8. Use humor to create a bond with your listener.
9. Be yourself.

YOUR CREDIT

There are two ways to legally purchase a car, a house or even a ticket to a movie theatre. You can pay cash for it or you can buy it on credit. Few things of any significant value in these United State are bought entirely with cash. To buy a house you need credit. To buy a new car you need credit. In some instances, to get a good job, you need good credit. Credit is a necessity in your life. You can't succeed without it. You really need it.

The problem with having credit is that so many people abuse it. Just as with a job, you will find that you can't get credit without a good credit history.

What is Credit?

Credit is the ability to buy or purchase items without paying for the entire cost of the item in cash. The person who sells you a product or service will allow you to purchase it without paying for it in cash.

Credit is someone's allowing you to buy what you want without paying all cash for it. This person or company will allow you to do this based upon their trust in you, your job history and your history of buying other products and services on credit from other businesses. You must first establish a good credit history to be allowed to purchase products and services on credit.

Sometimes, you may need to pay part of the cost of the item—from ten to twenty-five percent—in cash as a down payment, and owe the rest. If you have good credit, you won't have to pay anything down because the person selling you the item or lending you the money is confident, based on your previous credit purchases and your credit history, that you will pay the amount that you owe in regular installments.

The creditor will allow you to pay, over a period of time, the full amount for the item you purchased. You will be charged a fee for allowing you to make a purchase without paying cash for it. The fee is called interest.

How to Get Credit?

You have to start small. You will need to open a bank account and maybe a savings at your local bank. Next you have to fill out a credit application for the item that you want to purchase or for a line of credit.

Whenever you apply for credit, the lender will want to know where you live, where you work and where you bank. The longer you have lived or worked in the same place, the better your chance of getting that credit.

Don't apply for a major national credit card like Visa or MasterCard without first building up a good credit rating. Get "easier" forms of credit and pay off the bills on time for at least one year. Accounts at local department stores and accounts at certain mail order companies are easier forms of credit for beginners to get. They help you buy products at a particular store with a credit card that is good only at that store. Then you will be sent a bill.

The bill will give you the choice of paying the whole amount off in one payment within a few weeks and being charged no interest, or of paying a minimum amount each month—usually a percentage of the balance. You will then be charged a monthly interest on the balance you have not yet paid off.

Results

If you pay the minimum payment required every month and pay it on time, after a few months your credit rating will reflect your good payment record. Make sure that you don't miss a month. You could end up with a computerized credit rating indicating that you pay your debts late. This may prevent you from getting additional credit.

The Best Way to Get Credit

A useful method to build up your credit rating is to buy goods, such as furniture, televisions and a car, on a secured financing basis. In such a case, the store will sell you the items on credit, knowing that if you don't pay your monthly bill, they can legally take these items back from you.

As you pay for the items on a month-to-month basis, you are building up a good credit rating. Make sure that you are buying from a reputable store and that you know how much interest you are paying.

If you are turned down for credit at reputable stores, be careful how you choose other stores. Be extremely aware of and stay away from stores that offer you credit and then charge you high interest rates, and high late fee charges. Limit your monthly payments contracts to two years or less.

Don't buy something you don't need just to build your credit. But if you are already buying these products, consider this method of building your credit rating if the store is reputable.

Secured Borrowing

Auto and some other loans are usually made on a secured basis. This means that the bank can seize your car if you don't make your payments. They decrease their risk and will be more likely to give you credit without an extensive credit history if all your other information (where you live and where you work) is in order.

Keeping Good Credit

Once you build up your first credit accounts, you are ready to build up some really solid credit. The best thing to remember is to always pay at least your minimum payment on time every month. If you have a problem or grievance with the credit company, try to iron it out without holding back a payment.

If you maintain a good credit profile, you should be able to get more unsecured credit and credit cards with higher credit limits as time goes on.

YOUR DRIVER'S LICENSE

One of the most important privileges that you will obtain in your life is your driver's license. It is perhaps the hardest privilege to obtain, the easiest to lose and the hardest to get back

A driver's license is a right; it is a privilege granted to you by your state Department of Motor Vehicles (DMV). Don't take this lightly or without regards for the facts. Once you obtain your license and the privilege to own and operate a vehicle, you must always be on guard against losing this privilege.

What Your Drivers License Does for You

Your driver's license will give you the freedom and mobility that you need to go to work and school, to find a new and better job and to get back and forth to wherever you want to go. It is also a means of identification for such needs as credit card transactions, to obtain credit and to prove that you are you — your identity.

If you lose this privilege, you'll lose all this and you'll be catching the bus. You will have to depend on friends for a ride and or you'll be walking again. Just imagine losing your driving privilege and having to take your date out on the bus or in an expensive taxicab — if you can get one. This is one tool of your life that you must protect.

How to Get a Drivers License

If you are a resident of your state and 16 and over, you can get a driver's license by doing the following:

- Visit your state Department of Motor Vehicles office.
- Complete an application form.
- Provide your social security number.
- Verify your birth date and legal residence.

- Some states require a thumbprint.
- Pay the application fee.
- Pass a written traffic laws and sign test. You may only be allowed three (3) chances to pass.
- Have your picture taken.
- Obtain a learner's permit. It may take six months to one year before you are issued a driver's license.
- Pass a vision exam.
- Pass a driving test.
- Provide proof of automobile insurance.

In many states, if you are eighteen years or younger, you will have to provide proof that you:

- Completed driver education or driver training in an accepted driving school.
- Once you pass your written test, you will be issued a provisional (learner's) permit.
- A parent, guardian, spouse or adult 25 years or older who has a valid state driver's license must be with you when you drive a motor vehicle with a learner's permit. It is illegal for you to drive alone and without a licensed adult. If you are caught doing this, your driving privilege will be suspended.

Learners Permit License

- You cannot drive anyone under the age of twenty years at anytime during the first twelve months.
- You cannot drive between 11 pm and 5 am for the first twelve months.
- If you are under the age eighteen, you may not be employed to drive a motor vehicle.

How to Lose a Drivers License

- Drinking and driving under the influence of alcohol.
- Using drugs while operating a motor vehicle.
- Driving above the speed limit.
- Racing.
- Causing the death of another driver or occupants of either car in an accident that is your fault.

- Committing such traffic violations as running red lights, speeding, road rage, not using a seat belt, and so on.
- Not having the required car insurance.
- Failing to pay tickets or fines.
- Multiple accidents.
- Running from police.
- Not stopping on police commands.
- Not showing respect for your fellow driver.
- Driving without having your license document with you.
- Doing anything stupid.

It is hard to get your driving privilege and so easy to lose it. You need your driver's license to succeed in your job, to enjoy your personal relationships, and to experience personal growth. Think before you put your license in jeopardy. The state is not very forgiving and things will go downhill once you lose your license.

FINDING MY CAREER AND LIFE PURPOSE

Before proceeding to the next section of this book, take this test to insure that you understand what you just read and discussed. Put a check mark beside your answer to each question.

1. What is life all about?
   ( ) Competition against others for money.
   ( ) Competition against yourself and your mind.
   ( ) Having fun.
2. The value of the race in life lies in . . .
   ( ) going to the Super Bowl.
   ( ) the finish line of achieving a goal.
   ( ) in finishing what you start out to do.

3. Financial success is achieved by . . .
   ( ) people who do the same successful tasks over and over again.
   ( ) people who play the lotto.
   ( ) people who are lucky.
4. What are some of your choices in life after high school?
   ( ) Playing in the NBA or NFL.
   ( ) Getting an education or going into the military.
   ( ) Being a bum and just giving up on life.
5. What is your primary purpose for obtaining an education?
   ( ) To learn skills that you can offer to others for income.
   ( ) To get work skills to survive.
   ( ) Both of the above.
6. Where can you find work?
   ( ) The Sunday newspaper classified ads.
   ( ) Internets job websites.
   ( ) Friends and family members.
   ( ) All of the above.
7. Your résumé is important because . . .
   ( ) it will get you a job.
   ( ) it has to convince a potential employer to interview you.
   ( ) it makes you look good.
8. The quickest way to eliminate yourself from being considered for a job is to:
   ( ) not show up for the interview.
   ( ) be inappropriately dressed and poorly groomed.
   ( ) be shy during the interview.
9. Which nonverbal actions should you use at a job interview?
   ( ) Laugh out loud when there is a joke.
   ( ) Slap the interviewers on the back when you meet them.
   ( ) Maintain eye contact.
10. What is credit?
   ( ) The ability to buy without paying all cash.
   ( ) What you get for passing a school class.
   ( ) Acknowledgement for doing something right.
11. Is your driver's license a privilege?
   ( ) Yes.
   ( ) No.

Chapter Four

Dress for Business Success

THE WORLD'S DRESS CODE FOR MEN

Surviving day-to-day life is hard. The last thing that you want to do is to go against the grain of society. You want to do what you know will work to help you to develop a successful career and to earn income (money) to buy all the things that you want. Then why in the world would you do something like dress inappropriately for work, if it can stop you from making money?

Looking like a thug is not going to pay your bills or buy you a car. Weird hairstyles are not going to move you up the ladder to a higher income. Re-

member, these are fads that come and go in time. Next year—even next month—today's fads will be gone and some other fads or styles will become the new, hip way to dress.

As you get older, you will lose touch with fads—you should. You'll learn to dress like men—appropriately—so you won't offend potential customers who could give you money for your products and/or services. That is what it is all about at this period of your life.

You are out of high school now and probably working in the real world. Who cares how hip you are or if you are up-to-date with the latest style? Nobody really cares. All the world cares about is the bottom line, money. And what you have to offer. This is especially true for the girls who you are trying to impress with your stylish clothes and hair.

CLOTHES TO WOO THE LADIES

Now that you are in the real world, people are more concerned with what you have going for you: money, a job, a place to live and how you look, and how you act—in that order of importance. The world revolves around " What can you do for me?" and not "what can I do for you?"

If you have stylish clothes, eventually they'll go out of style. Somebody will come up with something new that "everybody" is wearing and you'll have to go buy this too. This will go on and on until you can't afford to continue, "staying in style." Even then, this won't guarantee that you will get the ladies because, at this stage of their lives, they aren't looking for someone who is in-style; they are looking for someone with some substance—money, a place to live, and a job.

I can be out of style and clean-cut, and (all else being equal) still get more ladies than you. How? If I have a good education, I can get a better job; I can make more money than you; I can buy a better car than you; I can get my own apartment; and I can take the ladies out to nice places to eat.

What can you do if you are spending all your money on clothes to keep in style? Looking stylish is no prerequisite for success with the ladies in the adult world. Get over it. You are not a teenager anymore.

If you are busy trying to keep up with the latest styles and fads you may neglect the other things that you need to offer a woman. Then you'll be faced with a life of one-night stands with the type of woman that you really should avoid. Such a woman will use you for her needs and when you are all used up, she'll dump you for someone who can offers her more than what you can offer.

If you are looking for a nice lady, someone to commit to and to have a relationship with, you should have the total package: a job, a car, a place of your own, and the ability to take her out and entertain her. Of course, you have to be compatible with her. I didn't say sex, because sex is next to the last requirement for success with the ladies. At the bottom of the list for most ladies is your wearing the latest clothing and hair fads, because nice ladies just want someone who dresses appropriately for the occasion.

CLOTHES FOR WORK

There is an old saying that clothes make the man. This is true. Your clothes are the first projection of who you are to other people. At first glace, people can interpret what you are all about. Your clothing choices in the adult world are a basic part of how you present yourself to the world. They speak for you, so it's important to choose carefully what you want them to say.

There is nothing more beautiful then a man in a perfectly tailored suit, with a formal dress shirt, a matching tie and polished shoes. Should you dress like this all of the time? Of course not, but clothing does make a statement about who you are or who you want to be.

Someday, you'll have to learn the language of adult clothing if you want to succeed in the business world. So it is a good idea to practice now. Sure there are movie actors, computer genius and rappers who get respect even if they dress like bums, geeks and thugs, but they are the exception to the rule.

Most adults dress in clothes that show intent. Wearing a tie, dress shirt and business attire shows that you are serious about your job or about getting a job. It also implies that you care about the way you look and how you project yourself to other. Dressing for success portrays an attitude; it tells the world who you are and who you want to be.

If you look like a thug, people will think you are a thug. If you dress like you don't care, then people will know that. If you dress like a bum and have dirty, smelly hair, guess what? There is another old saying, "You are what you eat." Let's extend that further, you are what people see that you clothes project you to be. People know.

DRESS CODES FOR WORK

You are not a teenager anymore. You are an adult in the real world. Stop playing games with yourself. People are not concerned about your hang-up, beliefs or baggage. All that is important right now is that you work and pay your own way.

At work, your supervisor does not want you to bring your problems to the job. He does not want you to force your lifestyle on your co-workers. He does not have to accept you, your attitudes or your opinions. He can get rid of you at any time. He can fire you. And guess what? Someone will replace you and be happy to have your job and make the money that you no longer will be earning.

You should follow these basic rules for dressing for work:

- It is very important to check with your supervisor on what is appropriate and what is not appropriate to wear on your job.
- Be safe. Dress appropriately and do not disrupt or interfere with the focus of your job in any way.
- Use deodorant and take a bath or shower every day before coming to work.
- Keep your hair cut and neatly trimmed at all times.
- Brush your teeth and gargle with Listerine, especially if you have been out-drinking the night before or if you are a smoker.
- Wear clean clothes every day. If you smoke or if you live with a smoker, make sure that your clothes are not giving off the smell of tobacco.
- Do not wear fad clothing or lifestyle clothing to work. Dress according to what is appropriate for your type of work.
- Do not wear clothing that is vulgar, obscene, and libelous or denigrates others on account of race, color, religion, gender, and so on.
- Do not wear excessive jewelry, earrings, nose rings, or fad jewelry to the job.
- Do not wear clothing that supports any cause, including the use of alcohol or drugs or illegal and violent activities.

GROOMING FOR WORK

Please don't forget the details that ensure your attractiveness as a total person. Good grooming is key to a successful image. Here is a grooming checklist:

1. Your hair should be clean and neat.
2. Your teeth should be brushed and you should have good breath.
3. Make sure that your deodorant is still working.
4. Shave your face and try to reduce the amount of hair on your face.
5. Keep your fingernails clean and filed.
6. Wear clean and neatly pressed clothes at all times.
7. Wear shirt cuffs and collars without frays.
8. Keep your shoes polished and without worn heels.
9. Do not wear excessive jewelry, earrings, nose rings, or fad jewelry to work.
10. Do not wear clothing to support any cause, including the use of alcohol or drugs, or which encourage illegal or violent activities.

Mix that with a great haircut, a neat and clean appearance, and you have it all. Now you can put your foot forward and make some money.

DRESS FOR BUSINESS SUCCESS

Before proceeding to the next section of this book, take this test to insure that you understand what you just read and discussed. Put a check mark beside your answer to each question.

1. Dressing inappropriately at work will . . .
   ( ) stop you from making money.
   ( ) make you stand out from others.
   ( ) make you look smart.
2. The world revolves around . . .
   ( ) what you can do for me.
   ( ) what I can do for you.
   ( ) what you do.
3. A total male package should include . . .
   ( ) a job.
   ( ) a car.
   ( ) a place to live on your own.
   ( ) all of the above.

4. Dressing appropriately at work makes a statement about . . .
    ( ) who you are.
    ( ) how much money you have.
    ( ) your taste for clothes.
5. When considering what to wear to work, you should . . .
    ( ) check with your supervisor.
    ( ) wear what you want.
    ( ) ask other employees what you should wear.
6. If you smoke . . .
    ( ) spray on cologne before work.
    ( ) ignore the smells.
    ( ) make sure that your clothes and breath are not giving off a tobacco smell.
7. Wearing fad clothing at work makes you . . .
    ( ) look good.
    ( ) show that you are up with the latest style.
    ( ) may not be appropriate for your work situation.
8. Use deodorant . . .
    ( ) when you smell odors given off by your body.
    ( ) every day before coming to work.
    ( ) to impress the girls at work.
9. Nose rings at work are . . .
    ( ) cool.
    ( ) in style.
    ( ) inappropriate to wear to work.
10. Your supervisor . . .
    ( ) wants you to force your lifestyle on others.
    ( ) thinks you dress cool.
    ( ) can fire you for dressing inappropriately at work.

About the Author

D. Harold Greene is the Executive Director of *Faith Institute of Entrepreneurship*, a non-profit corporation dedicated to improving the lives of at-risk males, as well as those of mature adults. The company publishes life-skill and self-sufficiency books and other information that will help people to become successful and self-sufficient.

Mr. Greene teaches continuing education courses and entrepreneurship training at numerous community colleges in the metropolitan Washington, D.C. region. This book, *The Rites of Passage for Males Manual*, is the centerpiece of a workshop to teach youth trainers, teachers, advisors, and mentors how to teach young men life-skills and self-sufficiency skills. He has developed "the Rites of Passage for Males Trainers Workshop" to teach life-skills and self-sufficiency training methods to youth trainers, teachers, and counselors. His workshop has been held in Maryland and North Carolina.

He has also developed an entrepreneurship-training manual, "50 Best Home Based Businesses for People Over 50" and a workshop of the same name. This workshop teaches mature and retired adults how to start home-based businesses.

Mr. Greene is an entrepreneur, a business consultant, a junior college lecturer, youth trainer, author, and publisher of self-help manuals and entrepreneurship publications.